Shopping

Activities for 3–5 Year Olds

Caroline Quin

Brilliant
PUBLICATIONS

We hope you enjoy using this book. If you would like further information on other titles published by Brilliant Publications, please write to the address given below or look on our website: www.brilliantpublications.co.uk.

Other books in the Activities for 3–5 Year Olds series:

All About Us	Gardening
Caring and Sharing	Pets
Colours	Weather
Families	Water
Food	

Published by Brilliant Publications,
Unit 10, Sparrow Hall Farm, Edlesborough, Bedfordshire, LU6 2ES
website: www.brilliantpublications.co.uk

Written by Caroline Quin
Second edition revised and updated in 2012 by Debbie Chalmers
Illustrated by Kirsty Wilson

© Caroline Quin 1999
Printed ISBN 978 0 85747 666 1
ebook ISBN 978 0 85747 081 2

The Publisher accepts no responsibility for accidents arising from the activities described in this book.

First published 1999. Second edition 2012
10 9 8 7 6 5 4 3 2 1

Contents

To avoid the clumsy 'he/she', the child is referred to throughout as 'he'.

Introduction

Most children go to the shops and comparing shopping experiences, with each other and with the adults, can provide an ideal theme for a project within an early years setting.

Talking about shopping and going shopping provides lots of opportunities for communication and language development and children can learn new vocabulary if they are introduced to the names for individual shops, such as ironmongers, estate agents, butchers and bakeries. They may understand the value of developing literacy skills if they help to write lists before leaving for the shops, and, whilst there, see a variety of signs and labels to read. Learning about the different shops, where they are and what they sell, supports the children's need to develop a greater understanding of the world, while handling and managing money provides opportunities for simple sums and developing skills in mathematics. The strength, endurance and stamina required to lift and carry heavy bags of shopping contributes to children's physical development and displaying consideration for other shoppers, while queuing, waiting and taking turns, develops personal, social and emotional development skills.

Set up different types of shops in the role-play area, such as a jeweller, a travel agency, a pet shop, a hairdresser or a garden centre. Involve the children at every stage and encourage them to decide on their own scenarios and to play cooperatively and imaginatively. It is worth investing in good quality toy tills and play money that will last and add some realism to the children's games. Other props can be easily provided from within the setting, donated by children's famiilies or made by the children themselves.

The activities in this book are linked to the Early Learning Goals of the Department for Education's revised *Statutory Framework for the Early Years Foundation Stage* (September 2012), and its guidance document, *Development Matters*. They recognize that children learn actively through playing and exploring, creating and thinking critically. The role of an early years practitioner is to provide stimulating and challenging activities within an enabling environment. Ideas must be flexible enough to meet the needs of each individual as a unique child and to build upon the children's knowledge and interests to promote active learning. All of the activities in this book may be easily adapted to suit individual children or groups of any size.

Going shopping

Learning opportunities
* Developing speaking and listening skills within a familiar group
* Offering ideas, experiences and opinions on a theme

Links to the Early Learning Goals
* Communication and language – Listening and attention, Speaking

Equipment and resources
No special requirements.

Activity
Gather a small group of about six children together to talk about going out shopping. Ask the children what they and their families do when they are getting ready to go shopping. Mention getting money, shopping lists amd shopping bags ready and ask whether anyone takes a shopping trolley with them. Discuss the differences between shopping in summer and in winter, such as wearing coats or sun hats, buying hot drinks or ice creams, protecting food from rain or snow or hurrying home with frozen food before it warms up in the sun. Encourage children to think of different methods of transport that people use to go shopping, such as walking, cycling, driving or taking a bus. Ask them to suggest which shops they might go to, such as a supermarket or a greengrocer, a shoe shop or a newsagent.

Extension

Make a chart of the different methods of transport the children's parents use to go shopping.

Discussion

Talk specifically about safety while shopping. Remind children that they must not wander away from the adult they are with, that they must never go away with a person they do not know and that they must be very careful when walking near to or crossing roads.

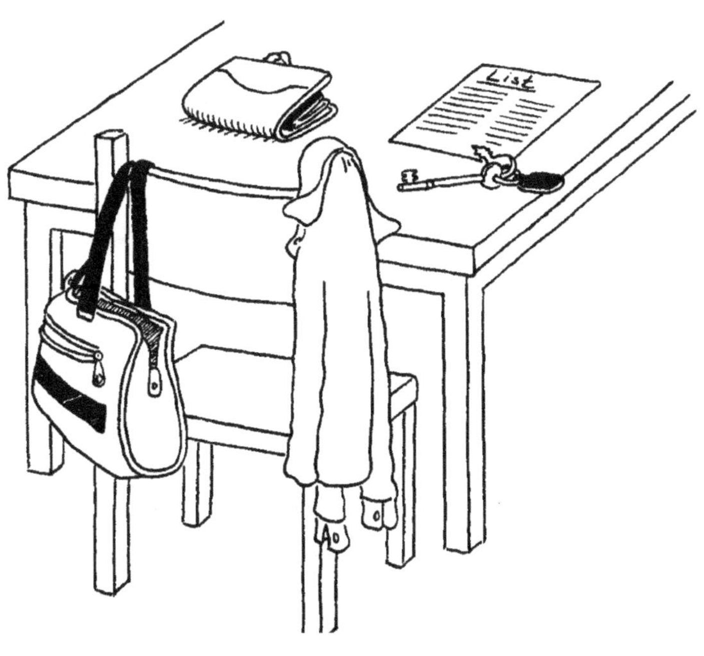

I went shopping and I bought ...

Learning opportunities
* Listening attentively, taking turns and speaking confidently within a familiar group
* Developing memory and imagination skills

Links to the Early Learning Goals
* Communication and language – Listening and attention, Understanding, Speaking

Also
* Personal, social and emotional development – Self-confidence and self-awareness, Making relationships

Equipment and resources
No special equipment.

Activity
Invite a small group of children to play a game. Begin by saying, 'I went shopping and I bought some apples.' Ask children in turn to repeat the line, but to choose a different item to buy. When they all understand and are confident, ask them to play by repeating each shopping item and adding a new one of their own. For example, the first child might say, 'I went shopping and I bought a bun.' The second child could then say, 'I went shopping and I bought a bun and some toothpaste.'

Extension

Play the game, asking children to choose new items
in alphabetical order, such as apples, bananas,
carrots, donkeys, elephants, etc. Allow the children
to be imaginative in their shopping choices. For an
alternative game, ask the children to think of rhyming
items to buy, such as custard and mustard or jellies
and wellies.

Discussion

Talk about ways of remembering, such as repeating
something to yourself time and time again or
association – thinking of the cat and remembering
cat food. When the children suggest impossible
ideas, such as buying an elephant, discuss why this
would usually be impossible and if there are any
circumstances in which it would be possible, such as if
you were the manager of a safari park or if you lived
in Africa.

A shopping story

Learning opportunities
* Developing listening, concentration and imaginative thinking skills
* Responding and adding to a group story
* Speaking confidently within a familiar group

Links to the Early Learning Goals
* Communication and language – Listening and attention, Understanding, Speaking

Also
* Expressive arts and design – Being imaginative

Equipment and resources
A zip-top shopping bag into which you can put a variety of shopping items, either based on a theme or items from particular shops, for example a necklace and a watch or a hat.

Activity
Invite a group of children to sit with you to take part in a discussion or make up a story. Start your story by saying, 'I went shopping this morning and I bought this (*getting an item from your bag*).' Ask the children what it is and at which type of shop you bought it. Repeat this for all the items in your bag and then, if you have based these on a theme, ask the children, 'What would you make with these?' or 'What links these items?'

Extension

Include various themes at different sessions, such as
cake ingredients, vegetables, pet foods, etc. Ask the
children to collect items from around the room from
which you and they can make up a story.

Discussion

Talk about and describe items bought in specialist
shops, such as from a haberdasher or a milliner.
Ask the children if they know what a shop that sells
medicine is called. Talk about how some specialist
shops have disappeared from our high streets and
how most items can now be bought under one roof –
in a chain store or supermarket.

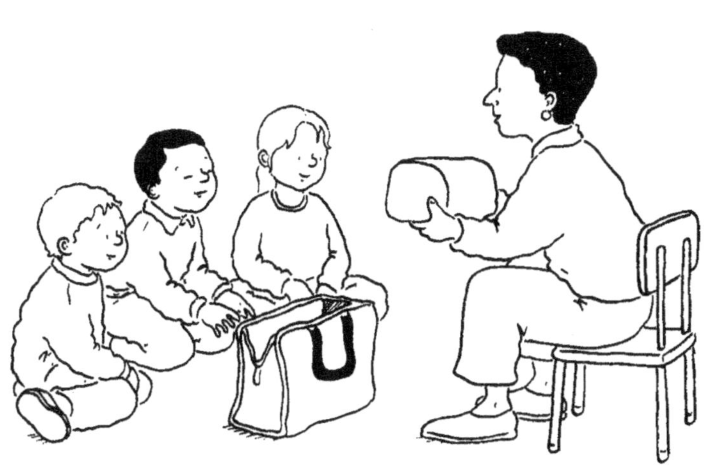

The clothes shop

Learning opportunities
* Practising independent dressing and undressing skills and manipulating various clothing fasteners

Links to the Early Learning Goals
* Physical development – Health and self-care

Equipment and resources
A variety of clothes and dressing up outfits in the correct sizes for the children; a clothes rail or another method of hanging the clothes (such as a broom handle balanced over two chairs); a surface on which to place folded clothes; a toy till and money or counters with a 'pay here' sign; areas to use as 'changing rooms'; safe bags and baskets to fill with clothes that have been purchased; at least one long mirror (either free standing or safely balanced against a wall).

Activity
Invite children to visit the role-play area and buy some clothes from the clothes shop. Adults should support the children in choosing different clothes and taking them into the changing rooms to try them on, encouraging them to put them on by themselves and to fasten them wherever possible. Zips and buttons may be demonstrated as necessary, while the children attempt to copy and learn to use them independently. Praise children for trying and persevering, whether they manage to fasten their own clothes or not. Encourage them to admire the style and ensure the fit

of their clothes by looking at themselves in the mirror.
If they do not like their selections, they may replace
them and choose others. They may take turns to be
shop assistants and customers and to pay for their
clothes at the till.

Extension

Provide accessories to go with the clothes, such as
scarves, gloves, handbags, belts, hats and jewellery.

Discussion

Talk with the children about how to make sure a new
item of clothing fits well. We need to check the length,
the waist, the width across the shoulders, the length
of the sleeves or legs, etc. Encourage children to think
about what colours of clothing they think suit them
and which colours they like to wear. Invite them to
share their real experiences of clothes shopping with
their families while talking to the group.

Run to the shops

Learning opportunities
* Running with care and co-ordination within a game, negotiating space and other people safely
* Transporting a variety of objects carefully and safely
* Following rules and instructions in order to participate in a group game

Links to the Early Learning Goals
* Physical development – Moving and handling
Also
* Communication and language – Understanding
* Personal, social and emotional development – Managing feelings and behaviour

Equipment and resources
A variety of items one could buy in a shop.

Activity
Invite children to sit in a group or a circle to play a game. Place a selection of 'shopping items' in another area of the room or garden. At least one adult should sit with the children and another with the props. Choose a child to begin the game and ask him to 'run to the shops' and fetch something for you. (This could be something beginning with a particular letter or sound, or something of a particular size or colour, or something from a particular shop, depending on the props that you have available). When the child brings the item back, ask the next child to 'run to the shops'

for another item. Allow each child to take a turn,
continuing until there are no more props left.

Extension

Make a careful selection of items for your shopping
table so that they all rhyme or relate to each other in
some way, perhaps by colour. Once a child has chosen
an item such as 'food for the cat', the next child could
get 'a new cricket bat'. Ask each child to go to the
shops in a different way – hop, skip, walk backwards.
Divide the children into two groups to play the game
simultaneously with different adults. With careful
planning and consultation, it may be possible to turn
the game into a race.

Discussion

Ask the children to think of times when they might
have to walk back from the shops very carefully,
such as if they were carrying a goldfish in a bowl or
some eggs in a paper bag, or if they were carrying
something very heavy and could not run with it.

A shopping exercise

Learning opportunities
* Improving control of whole body movements
* Developing mime and acting skills and using imagination

Links to the Early Learning Goals
* Physical development – Moving and handling
Also
* Expressive arts and design – Being imaginative

Equipment and resources
No special equipment.

Activity
With the children, act out going to the supermarket. Pretend to write a list of the things you need, then get into the car, drive to the shop and park there. Ask the children to collect a trolley and go into the shop. Pretend that the first section has fruit and vegetables and decide with the children what to buy. Remember to think of different weights and sizes and which are more delicate. (For example, don't put potatoes on top of mushrooms!) Act out buying items from other sections of the shop, such as meat, tinned foods, dairy produce and drinks. Take the trolley to the check out and unload all the shopping onto the conveyor belt. Ask children to try to remember all the things they bought. Take the shopping out to the car, load it in, drive home and unload it all into the house. Then mime sitting down for a drink and a biscuit!

Extension

Instead of going to the supermarket, go to the garden centre and carry out a similar exercise. Ask the children to contribute ideas about what they are going to buy.

Discussion

Ask the children whether they think that their trolleys would have been full with the things they pretended to buy (probably unlikely). Ask if they can remember what they bought during the game. Talk about how heavy or light the shopping is and how long it takes to get it all done.

Buying for a picnic

Learning opportunities
* Understanding how to contribute to a joint project within a group
* Developing confidence in making choices, offering and discussing ideas and opinions and being sensitive to the wishes and views of others

Links to the Early Learning Goals
* Personal, social and emotional development – Self-confidence and self-awareness, Making relationships

Also

* Communication and language – Speaking

Equipment and resources
A large piece of paper and pen; a small piece of paper and pen.

Activity
Plan a fairly simple picnic for the whole group and talk to the children about when it could be. Ask them where they think it should be held – in the garden, at the park or playground, or indoors if it is raining? Ask the children to contribute ideas to your shopping list. Write these ideas on the large sheet of paper and then later transfer to the smaller one.

Extension

This activity can be combined with shopping for other occasions, at any time of year, or with buying the ingredients for making cakes and biscuits to eat at the picnic. Support children as they unpack the shopping bags and check the items against the list you all prepared together.

Discussion

Help the children with their suggestions. If they say sandwiches, ask what kind and remember to add bread and butter to your list. If they suggest crisps –what flavour? If they suggest fruit – which type? Encourage them to help you transfer the big list to a smaller one as it would be impracticable to take the large sheet into the supermarket!

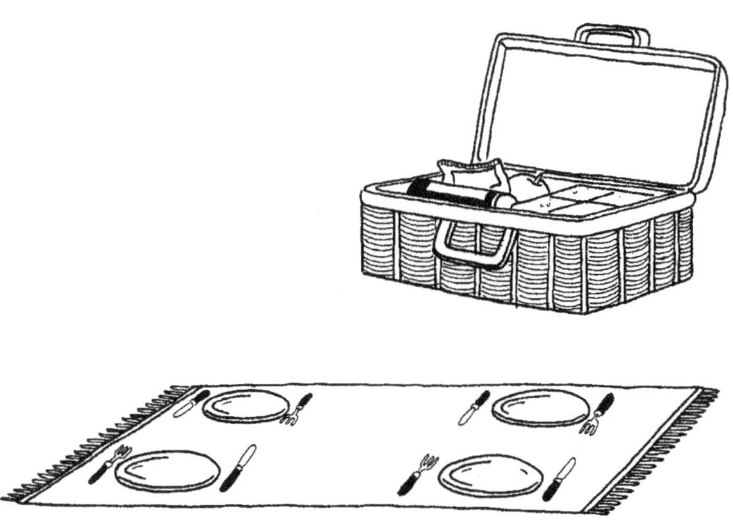

Shopping for Gran

Learning opportunities
* Developing an awareness and an understanding of how to help a relative or friend who is unable to carry out normal tasks due to an accident or illness

Links to the Early Learning Goals
* Personal, social and emotional development – Managing feelings and behaviour, Making relationships

Equipment and resources
No special equipment.

Activity

Discuss what might happen if Gran (or another relative, friend or neighbour) had, for example, fallen over and broken her ankle and it was in plaster. Suggest to the children that they might go to her house, with their parents, and try to help her and ask for ideas on how they could help. They might check whether she had somewhere comfortable to sit and rest her leg, whether she could reach her books or her knitting or sewing or turn the television on and off if she wanted to and whether she had enough to eat and drink. They could ask if she would like them to fetch anything for her, such as fish and chips for dinner, and whether they should arrange to eat them with her and then wash the dishes. Perhaps they could ask another friend or neighbour to call in later?

Extension

For example, perhaps she needs someone to fetch a prescription or to post a letter for her. Ask the children if they know where to go to do those things.

Discussion

Talk with the children about ways of helping all sorts of different people who are ill or disabled. Ask whether they know about any special provisions made to help disabled people to do their shopping, such as particular car parking spaces, trolleys that attach to wheelchairs, assistants who are willing to help within supermarkets and delivery services.

Setting up shop

Learning opportunities
* Playing cooperatively with others and working together to make decisions and create games
* Using experience and imagination to recreate a shop in the role-play area

Links to the Early Learning Goals
* Personal, social and emotional development – Making relationships

Also
* Expressive arts and design – Being imaginative
* Understanding the world – The world

Equipment and resources
A shop in the role-play area – tables or chairs to make counters and shelves, dressing up outfits or overalls for shop assistants, toy till, play money, paper and pens or pencils, scissors, old newspapers or scrap paper, items to 'sell' in the shop; shopping bags.

Activity
Encourage the children to discuss and plan the type of shop they would like to create first. (If they can't all agree on one, set up two shops side by side, plan different ones for different days of the week or create a 'general store' or a supermarket, that sells most things!) Adults and children can work together to make counters and shelves and set out items for sale. Demonstrate how to stuff boxes and bags with old paper to make them stable and more realistic if using,

for example, empty cartons and packets for a grocery. Encourage children to take turns to be shop assistants and customers and play with them, taking roles in the games too. Model appropriate behaviours and new vocabulary to extend the children's learning and their enjoyment of the activity

Extension

Have more than one shop at a time, perhaps a grocer's and a toy shop. Provide shopping trolleys or baskets. Make a 'scanner' such as supermarkets have at their check-outs.

Discussion

Talk about all the different jobs there are for people to do in shops and who might work in them as well as the sales assistants. Ask children to think about where all the things that are sold in shops originally come from.

Shopping lists

Learning opportunities
* Understanding how to make a shopping list to take to the supermarket and why one might be needed

Links to the Early Learning Goals
* Literacy –Writing

Equipment and resources
Large pen and paper for you; small pens and paper for the children.

Activity
Working with a maximum of two children at a time, tell them you are going to go to the supermarket to do your week's shopping. Ask them to help you compile your list. Encourage them to come up with the ideas, but give them clues such as – 'We seem to have only meat here. What else could we have for dinner?' Or, 'I have a pet. What sort of pet do you think I have? What does it need to eat?' As the children make their suggestions, write the list on your paper. If the children are able, let them write their own lists as well. If they cannot yet write letters or numbers, or spell words, ask them to make marks that can be understood as a shopping list, such as pictures of the items needed and groups of lines to indicate how many of each.

Extension

Make a set of cards showing pictures of a variety of
grocery items and another set of cards showing the
names of the items, such as 'baked beans' and 'eggs'.
Invite children to match the name cards with the
pictures, with adult support if needed.

Discussion

Talk about why a shopping list is useful. Suggest that
it helps you to remember the things you need and
discourages you from buying other things, that you
don't need. Ask children to think of other times at
which a list would be useful, such as when packing to
go on holiday.

A memory game

Learning opportunities

* Recognizing and matching pictures, shapes and names
* Remembering the positions of hidden pictures and words
* Following instructions, playing cooperatively and taking turns

Links to the Early Learning Goals

* Literacy – Reading

Also

* Communication and language – Understanding

Equipment and resources

Using white cardboard, make a pack of about 12 playing cards, fewer for younger children. Illustrate each card with a shopping commodity. Make a duplicate pack of cards with exactly the same pictures. You could choose a toy, a postage stamp, a can of pet food, a banana, etc.

Activity

Invite two or more children to play a 'Shopping Memory' game. Place one pack of cards face down, in front of the children, in a pile. Ask the children to spread out the duplicate pack, face up, and to take a good look at all the pictures and their positions before turning them over. Ask one child to take a card from the pile and look at it. Encourage the child to say which type of shop the item would come from and

then to look for the matching card. He may choose
one of the face down cards to turn over. If it matches,
he takes another turn. If not, he turns the card back
and the next child takes a turn.

Extension

Shuffle all the cards together and spread them all out,
face down. Ask children to choose and turn over two
cards at a time and see whether they match. Instead
of making two identical sets of picture cards, write
words such as 'butcher's shop', 'bakery', 'chemist' or
'supermarket' on one set and ask children to match
the words with the appropriate pictures.

Discussion

Name and talk about all the items and shops as the
cards are turned. Ask children if they can turn over a
specific item, such as 'a loaf of bread' or give verbal
clues, such as, 'I think the bananas are on the top row.'

The news-vendor

Learning opportunities
* Recognizing that people sometimes sell items, such as newspapers, from a stall or other place in a street or shopping centre
* Imagining and experiencing a different occupation and way of life
* Creating signs that give messages

Links to the Early Learning Goals
* Literacy – Reading, Writing
Also
* Understanding the world – The world

Equipment and resources
Large boxes, chairs or a table to make the stall; piles of newspapers; easels, notice boards or large pieces of cardboard to make signs; dressing up outfits for news-vendors; a bag of play money.

Activity
Work with the children to make a stall for a news-vendor. Ask them to make up news headlines and to write them on the boards and display them around the stall. If they can't think of ideas at first, suggest that they read some of the headlines in the old newspapers and adapt them. Pile the newpapers on the stall and make more piles on the floor. Encourage children to take turns to be news-vendors and customers, calling out the news and selling and buying papers.

Extension

Some news-vendors sell more than papers. They sell souvenirs, guides and maps. Embellish your stall with these too.

Discussion

Ask children to think about what clothes news-vendors usually wear and how they manage to continue when it rains or is very windy. You could suggest that the papers would need to have plastic covers or bricks to weigh them down. Ask whether the children's parents and carers buy newspapers from a vendor at a stall, go to a local shop, pick them up when they are in a supermarket or have them delivered. Talk with the children about whether both women and men become news-vendors and what special qualities you might need to be a good one (probably a loud voice and not minding being out of doors in all weathers).

Buying shoes

Learning opportunities
* Understanding how to measure the lengths and widths of feet and to fit shoes and why it is important to find and choose shoes of the right size

Links to the Early Learning Goals
* Mathematics – Shape, space and measures

Equipment and resources
Lots of spare pairs of shoes, for adults and children, lent or donated by staff and families; empty shoe boxes; mirror (large enough for looking at shoes, lent against a wall); rulers and tape measures; pieces of card with drawings of soles of shoes in different sizes to be used as foot measures. (Local shoe shops can be approached for help with children's projects and will often be able to donate empty shoe boxes and possibly lend commercial foot measures and shoe samples.)

Activity
Work with the children to set up a shoe shop in the role-play area. Play with the children, taking turns to buy and sell shoes. Encourage children to measure each other's feet and say which shoe sizes are needed, to try on different shoes and find out which fit and to compare the sizes of adults' and children's feet and shoes.

Extension

Draw around the children's and the adults' feet, order them by size, label them with names and display the pictures. Find and display pictures of shoes and other footwear from different eras and for different occupations and seasons.

Discussion

Encourage children to share their experiences of going to buy shoes with their families. Talk about the importance of having shoes that fit well, both in width and length, how much different types of shoes cost, how quickly children grow out of their shoes, while adults' shoes last longer, and the different fashions in shoes.

Buying shopping

Learning opportunities
* Matching, sorting and counting skills
* Understanding and using one-to-one correspondence and simple addition
* Understanding the concept of exchanging money for items and of a number of smaller coins or other items being equal to a larger one

Links to the Early Learning Goals
* Mathematics – Numbers, Shape, space and measures

Equipment and resources
Some items to buy spread out on a counter. Display empty packets such as egg boxes, fabric conditioner bottles, cornflake packets, tea packets (stuff thin cardboard boxes well to simulate that they are full); clear 'price' labels on each item; a large card that shows the value of the 'money'; a variety of large and small containers; a till or shoe box to use as a receptacle for the 'money'; counters.

Activity
Make a large chart which gives the value of the counters (2 small red counters = 1 large red counter; 3 small yellow counters = 1 large yellow counter; 4 small green counters = 1 large green counter; 5 small blue counters = 1 large blue counter). Give each child a mixed handful of counters. Invite children to take turns to be customers and shopkeepers, buying and selling items from the shop, using the correct

numbers of coloured counters. Offer support and encouragement as necessary, while children count, add and compare.

Extension
Make the money more complex by also making 10 yellow counters = 1 large red counter, etc.

Discussion
Discuss how money can be exchanged for goods. Talk about different forms of paying for goods, such as credit cards and cheques.

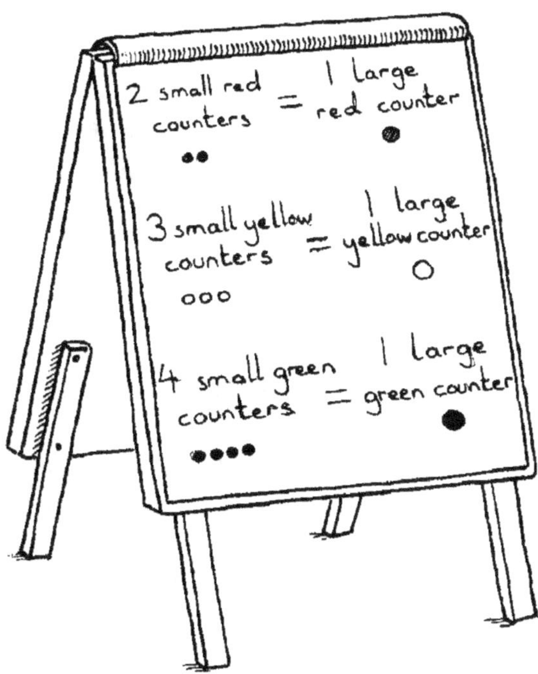

Is your purse empty?

Learning opportunities
* Matching and counting skills
* Simple addition and subtraction
* Understanding how to use money and plan spending within a budget

Links to the Early Learning Goals
* Mathematics – Numbers, Shape, space and measures

Equipment and resources
Four shopping baskets (made out of the insides of household matchboxes, with handles stapled across them); a die; at least 30 counters/buttons per child; lots of pictures of shopping items cut out and glued onto cards (small enough to fit into the baskets).

Activity
Mark each picture with different numbers of dots, making each item have a value of between 1 and 6. For example, a watch might have 6 dots, but a tin of cat food only 1 dot. Playing with a maximum of four children at a time, divide the counters out equally. Each child, in turn, may throw the die and buy something that has a value equivalent to the number of dots shown, putting it into his shopping basket. As the game progresses, it increases in difficulty, as the children try to spend exactly the amount of money that they have left. The game ends when a child manages to spend his budget money exactly.

Extension

Include a rule that allows children to buy two items, instead of one, that equal the number on the die. For example, if a 6 is thrown, a child may choose an item with 4 dots and an item with 2 dots. Provide purses so that each child can keep their money in a purse.

Discussion

Talk about adding the prices of items together, the costs of shopping and the real costs of different things.

Finding out the prices

Learning opportunities
* Understanding how to collect data and share it
  with the group
* Recognizing and recording numbers and adding
  them together

Links to the Early Learning Goals
* Mathematics – Numbers
Also
* Understanding the world – The world

Equipment and resources
A short shopping list (maximum six items), duplicated
for each child. Make sure the list is specific, so indicate
sizes and makes, such as 500g packet of Kellogg's
cornflakes, 415g can of Heinz baked beans.

Activity
Give each of the children a copy of the short shopping
list and explain to them (and to their parents and
carers) that you would like them to find out the price
of each of the items, if possible, when they next go
to a supermarket, and to write them down. Suggest
a realistic date by which all lists should be returned,
so that the information may be shared amongst the
group.

Extension

Ask the children to choose any one item of their own choice to add to their list and provide the price for that too.

Discussion

Talk with children about how they might carry out the activity. They will need to ask for help from an adult. The task could be carried out alongside the family shopping or on a separate journey. Explain that they must find each item themselves and then check with the adult to see that it is the right one. Praise and thank children and families who make efforts to complete the task, without drawing attention to those who were unable or unwilling to join in. Share the information collected and compare the costs of the items in different shops, encouraging children to think about which items and shops have prices that are more or less than others.

Packing the shopping

Learning opportunities
* Developing spatial awareness by packing smaller boxes and cartons into larger ones and fitting and stacking them together

Links to the Early Learning Goals
* Mathematics – Shape, space and measures
Also
* Physical development – Moving and handling

Equipment and resources
A variety of large cardboard boxes (such as fruit boxes with holes in them, shallow trays, taller and deeper cartons and strengthened wine carriers); a quantity of smaller boxes, tubs and cartons (such as those which have held cornflour, tomato purée, icing sugar, cereals, crackers, margarine, cake decorations, chocolates and frozen foods); plastic bottles (such as those for water, soft drinks and fabric conditioners). Reinforce any flimsy containers by padding them with paper and attach any loose lids or flaps firmly with sticky tape.

Activity
Invite children to choose a large box and try to fill it with smaller boxes, cartons and bottles, fitting them in together and packing it to the top without anything overflowing and falling out. Encourage them to guess how much will fit before they experiment and find out, and to decide whether they will need one box or two for a collection of items.

Extension

Let the children choose other things from around the room to pack and to find out whether they fit into the boxes with the shopping items.

Discussion

Wonder aloud whether all the cartons and bottles would fit into this or that box. Decide with the children whether some of the empty boxes are better for shopping than others and which is the best.

Ask how parents and carers usually pack their shopping and whether they use their own boxes or bags or supermarket carrier bags – or whether they just order it online and have it delivered!

The weight of things

Learning opportunities

* Understanding that measurement of weight does not change, but that size is not necessarily an indicator of weight, as different materials are heavier or lighter

Links to the Early Learning Goals

* Mathematics – Shape, space and measures

Equipment and resources

A set of clear scales; a variety of different items of shopping that are the same and different weights, for example, tea, sugar, pasta, flour, breakfast cereal, washing powder, cotton wool balls, disposable nappies, bags of crisps.

Activity

This activity will demonstrate to children that the weight of an item cannot necessarily be guessed from its size. A kilogram bag of sugar, reasonably compact, is the same weight as a kilogram packet of cornflakes although their size will differ considerably. Spread out the collection of shopping items and invite a pair or small group of children to lift each item and feel how much it weighs. Ask them to decide which is heavier and which is lighter and to try to line them up in order of weight. Invite them to use the scales and to weigh each item to find out whether they are right. Encourage them to discuss their findings and apply their own logic to understanding why some items are heavier than others.

Extension

Tell the children that 500 grams is equal to half a kilogram. Show them where the weight is printed on the items. Make a chart of what is heaviest and what is lightest.

Discussion

Some things that are big are not necessarily heavy. Conversely, some things that are small may not be light. Talk about the different types of scales that the children may have seen, such as those that are used in a baby clinic and those that are used in a supermarket.

Catalogue items

Learning opportunities
* Developing an understanding of the ways in which
  items are linked to each other and grouped together
* Describing shapes, sizes and characteristics,
  similarities and differences

Links to the Early Learning Goals
* Understanding the world – The world
Also
* Mathematics – Shape, space and measures

Equipment and resources
Catalogues and magazines; scissors; PVA glue and
spreaders; large pieces of paper with the names of
different types of shops on them (and picture clues if
the children are not yet readers); spare paper (to add
further shops of the children's choice).

Activity
Invite children to choose pages of items from
catalogues and magazines and to cut out the pictures.
Encourage them to decide which shops their items
would be sold in, or to look for items that would be
sold in specific shops, and to stick the pictures onto
the appropriate pieces of paper.

Extension

Provide a wide selection of three-dimensional shopping items, such as a packet of rice, a teddy or toy, a necklace, a newspaper, etc. Label tables or sheets of paper with the types of shops in which these would be bought and ask the children to sort and group the objects and take them to the right shops.

Discussion

Decide with the children which shops sell all sorts of different things, such as supermarkets, garden centres and DIY shops, and which sell only one type of thing, such as butchers and fishmongers or clothes and shoe shops.

Shopping 'Kim's game'

Learning opportunities
* Understanding similarities and differences and the ways in which items are linked to each other and grouped together
* Identifying the 'odd one out' within a group or collection

Links to the Early Learning Goals
* Understanding the world – The world

Equipment and resources
A tray; a tea towel, cloth or piece of fabric to cover the tray; a selection of items that could come from one particular shop and one item that obviously would not. (For example, a carrot, an onion, an apple, some grapes and a shoe.)

Activity
Invite a small group of children to sit around the covered tray. Explain to the children that the cover will be lifted off for 20 seconds (or for however long you choose), so that they can look carefully and memorize the items in order to say what is on the tray and which is the odd one out. Remove the cover for the specified time, then replace it and ask the children about the items on the tray. Encourage them to describe the odd one out.

Extension

Play the game with more items, up to a maximum of
seven altogether. Allow less time for the children to
memorize it, say, 15 then 10 seconds, telling them each
time you have reduced the time involved.

Discussion

Talk with the children about where they might be
able to purchase the items on the tray and why one is
obviously the odd one out. There may be reasons why
a different item could also be considered an odd one
out. Listen to the children's reasoning and encourage
their ideas. If they cannot remember all of the items
on the tray, offer clues to help them. (If none of the
groups can remember them all, reduce the number of
items until they become more practised at the game.)

Where do you shop?

Learning opportunities
* Developing an awareness and an understanding that people have different needs and preferences and may make differing choices or change their minds regularly when making decisions to suit their families
* Understanding how to collect data from people in order to carry out research and make comparisons

Links to the Early Learning Goals
* Understanding the world – People and communities

Also
* Mathematics – Shape, space and measures

Equipment and resources
A large piece of paper ruled into columns and boxes under each of the various local supermarket names: Co-op, Iceland, Morrison's, Safeway, Sainsbury's, Tesco, Aldi, Asda, Waitrose, etc; a list of the names of all of the children in the group; coloured pens and/or stickers.

Activity
Gather the children together and explain the chart you have made and the data that you are going to collect. Speak to each child individually, during a free play session, to ask where her family usually does most of their household and food shopping. Invite children to colour in a box or place a sticker in the appropriate

column. Ask them to write their names there or to
make a mark while you scribe for them. Having asked
each child you should have achieved a complete
clear bar chart in bright colours. Sometimes you will
find that people use more than one supermarket on
a regular basis. Find a way of indicating this on your
chart. Perhaps if Sheena's mum uses Iceland and
Tesco, you could outline the whole square on each
column, but only colour in half of the square.

Extension
Add an extra column for children whose parents
do not use a supermarket but prefer to shop at
local individual shops. Ask the children to bring in
examples of the packaging of 'own brands' sold by the
supermarkets.

Discussion
Talk about the different ways that families may use to
get to the supermarket and how much they can carry
if they don't take a car. Ask whether they have visited
any of the supermarkets slightly further away or in
other places and what differences they have noticed.
Talk about using smaller, local shops as well as the
larger ones.

Pop to the shops

Learning opportunities
* Understanding how to carry out a particular errand in order to help someone else
* Planning when and how to go out and what needs to be taken
* Considering necessary care and safety measures during the outing

Links to the Early Learning Goals
* Understanding the world – People and communities, The world

Equipment and resources
Shopping list; purse or wallet with money; a shopping bag; one adult for every two children.

Activity
Explain to the children that you have offered to run an errand for an old lady who lives next door to you. Choose two children to help you on this occasion, and reassure the others that they may help on another occasion soon. Tell them what you have to buy, for example milk, tea, biscuits. Count the money out and put it in a purse. Ask one child to take care of the purse and the other to carry the shopping bag. When at the shop, let them look for or ask for the commodity, then let them pay for it and help them count the change.

Extension

Take photographs of the children at the shops,
including some of them actually doing the
purchasing. Display the photographs. Go into more
than one shop and buy several things. Ask the
children to help you remember what it is you want to
purchase.

Discussion

Talk about road safety, the Green Cross Code,
staying beside an adult and using zebra and pelican
crossings whenever possible. Remind the children
of all the responsibilities involved in buying an item
of shopping, such as taking the money carefully,
going to the right shop, finding the item, paying for
it, checking your change and bringing the item and
money home safely. Emphasize the importance of
telling someone where you are going and what you
will be doing, once you are old enough to go out
alone.

Alternative ways of shopping

Learning opportunities
* Using technology to shop for, order and pay for items 'online'

Links to the Early Learning Goals
* Understanding the world – Technology

Equipment and resources
Catalogues; computer; calculators; paper and pens.

Activity
Look through catalogues with the children and choose two or more items that the setting needs to buy. It could be new toys or pieces of equipment, or just the next regular order of paper and sand. Show them how to write down the catalogue numbers and how many of each item they need so that they can make an order. Support them in typing the prices into a calculator and adding them together to find out the total cost. Read out the website address from the catalogue and demonstrate how to type the right letters into the computer to find it and then the numbers of the items you would like to order. Allow children to take turns to type in some letters and numbers, under adult supervision, but ensure that they are only watching while an adult completes and sends the order. Try to ensure that the order will arrive while the children are present at the setting and invite the courier or delivery

person to show them the hand-held machine used to
record the parcel's safe arrival.

Extension

Ask children to suggest ideas and, together, make a
list of other alternative ways of buying things, such
as: Internet sales (from ordering groceries online
to buying products from Amazon or ebay; at the
door (windows, vegetables, household articles); by
telephone (insurance, catalogue items); from rounds
vans (ice cream, fish); charity shops, village fetes,
car boot sales and jumble sales (second-hand goods
and handmade craft items); farms and markets (fresh
produce and preserves). Ask the children which of
these ways of shopping they have experienced.

Discussion

Talk about the different ways in which people have
bought and exchanged things in the past. Explain
the barter system and how people have used various
articles, such as pebbles, shells and jewels, in the way
we now use coins and
paper notes. Mention
that, in some countries,
it is quite normal to
'haggle' over prices,
rather than pay what
is asked, especially in
markets. Ask whether
any of the children,
or their families, have
visited such countries
on holiday and bought
souvenirs in this way.

Our shopping parade

Learning opportunities
* Using experience and imagination to decide which
  shops to include in a shopping parade

Links to the Early Learning Goals
* Understanding of the world – The world
Also
* Literacy – Writing

Equipment and resources
A variety of empty cardboard boxes of similar
proportions (at least one for each child); paints in a
variety of colours (mixed with PVA glue if the boxes
are shiny); a long strip of wallpaper or lining paper.

Activity
With the children, decide upon the types of shop they
would like to have in a shopping parade. Some of
them can occur more than once, as competition, such
as clothes shops, estate agents and banks. Invite the
children to paint the wallpaper in grey and brown, to
make a road and pavements, and to paint the boxes as
they wish, with shop fronts and signs. When the shops
are completed, the children can stick them to the road.

Extension

The shopping parade could be embellished with people made out of pipe cleaners and with trees made out of cotton wool balls, screwed-up paper fixed on lolly sticks or twigs stuck into Plasticine®. Little cars could be placed on the road.

Discussion

Ask children what their shops sell and whether any of them sell a mixture of goods. For example, a post office may also sell ice creams, sweets, groceries, cards, envelopes and newspapers. Offer new vocabulary on the theme, such as a shoe mender being called a 'cobbler' or a fish and chip shop being known as a 'takeaway'. Talk about any shops that have not yet been made and decide whether they should be added to the shopping parade.

The baker's shop

Learning opportunities
* Using malleable materials to create role-play items to sell in a baker's shop
* Using experience and imagination in planning and design

Links to the Early Learning Goals
* Expressive arts and design – Exploring and using media and materials, Being imaginative

Also

* Physical development – Moving and handling

Equipment and resources
Dough made from equal quantities of plain flour and salt; rolling pins; pastry cutters; spare flour; pictures of bread, bread rolls, cakes, tarts, sausage rolls, Cornish pasties, sandwiches, Swiss rolls, cream horns, etc; powder paint; PVA glue; cotton wool balls or tissue.

Activity
Suggest to the children that you could set up a baker's shop in the role-play area and that they could make play items to sell in the shop. Offer the salt dough and pictures and model skills such as rolling out, cutting out and moulding shapes. Leave the 'food' to dry in a warm place, such as the bottom of an airing cupboard or on top of a radiator, for at least a week. The thicker items will take longer to dry. Explain to the children that the dough will dry hard, but that it will take time.

Extension

Paint the bakery items appropriately, using powder paint mixed with PVA glue. Decorate cream cakes with cotton wool or tissue.

Discussion

Ask children whether their families buy food from baker's shops or from the bakery sections in supermarkets. Talk about the types of things that are sold in bakeries and whether the local baker has a machine for slicing bread, filled rolls and sandwiches and birthday cakes. Ask children to try to remember or imagine the smell of a bakery.

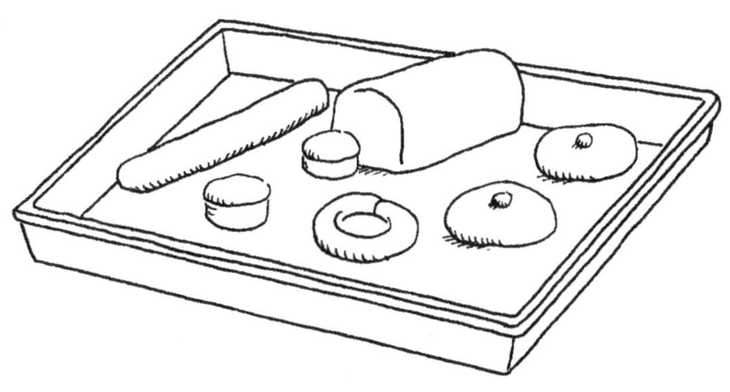

Bus to the shops

Learning opportunities
* Using recycled and craft materials to create a large model of a bus
* Manipulating tools and materials
* Working cooperatively within a group

Links to the Early Learning Goals
* Expressive arts and design – Exploring and using media and materials, Being imaginative

Also
* Physical development – Moving and handling
* Personal, social and emotional development – Making relationships

Equipment and resources
Several huge cardboard boxes (for example for televisions); big crayons, extra large felt-tipped pens or paint with household-size brushes; PVA glue; black white and coloured papers; sticky tape and masking tape; scissors.

Activity
Ask the children to help you make a bus from the cardboard boxes. Encourage them to decide how to fit and join the boxes together and then to colour them and make windows, doors, signs, numbers, wheels, passengers, etc to glue on. Leave the bus to dry. Provide dressing up outfits for bus drivers, conductors and passengers, play money, machines and change bags, paper for tickets and chairs to be the seats.

Encourage children to take turns to play the different roles and act out journeys to various places.

Extension

Add seats by putting little chairs in the bus. Fashion a steering wheel and attach it to the front (a paper plate does well for this, with a tube from a kitchen roll). Carefully cut a door and windows in the bus using a Stanley knife (out of the view of the children) before commencing the activity.

Discussion

Ask the children who they think will use the bus and where they will go, sharing ideas to encourage imagination. Ask whether they use buses with their families, where they go and whether they have to buy their ticket from a machine before boarding the bus or if the bus has a conductor or driver who takes the fares.

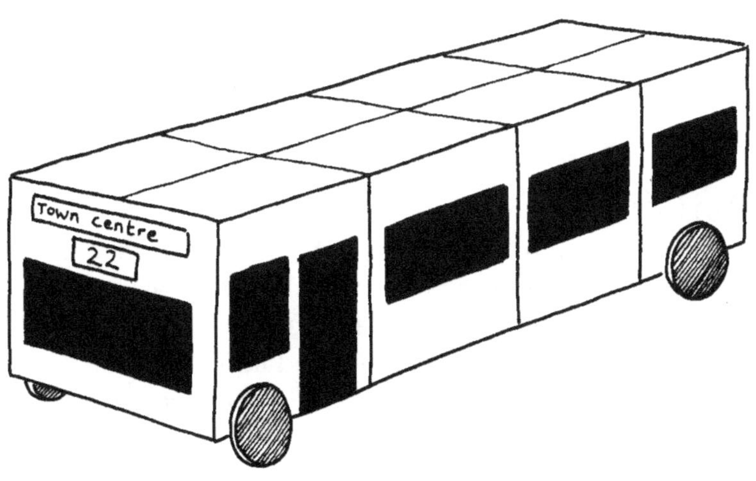

The café

Learning opportunities

* Using experience and imagination to recreate a café situation in the role-play area
* Developing an awareness of people's different opinions, needs and preferences
* Playing cooperatively with others

Links to the Early Learning Goals

* Expressive arts and design – Being imaginative

Also

* Understanding the world – People and communities
* Personal, social and emotional development – Making relationships

Equipment and resources

A café in the role-play area – tables and chairs, tablecloths, flowers, cups and saucers, plates, trays, play food, dressing-up outfits or aprons for café staff, notepads and pens or pencils, a counter area, toy till, play money.

Activity

Invite children to play in the café, taking turns to take on the roles of waiters and waitresses and various customers. Adults can play with the children, modelling appropriate actions and language. As waiters and waitresses, they will take orders, serve food, clear the tables and take money. As customers, they will order food and pretend to eat it and pay for it.

Extension

Also use the café area to serve real food at snack times. The children could make real sandwiches, biscuits or bowls of fruit or vegetables as a separate activity and then take them to the café and serve them to each other or the adults as customers.

Discussion

Ask children to share their experiences of eating out with their families. Talk about the different types of restaurants and cafés that they might have been to and the different foods and drinks that are served.

Packet models

Learning opportunities
* Designing and creating models using recycled and craft materials
* Improving skills in handling basic tools and equipment
* Control and coordination of small movements

Links to the Early Learning Goals
* Expressive arts and design – Exploring and using media and materials, Being imaginative

Also
* Physical development – Moving and handling
* Communication and language - Speaking

Equipment and resources
A quantity of clean, empty cartons, packets and boxes from shopping, such as tea packets, toothpaste boxes, pizza packs, soap boxes, egg cartons, etc; PVA glue; spreaders; scissors; pens; sticky tape and masking tape; paint and brushes.

Activity
Encourage children to sort and discuss the boxes and cartons before they start to use them. The children could sort by size or by what the boxes held, or they could decide on their own criteria for sorting. Invite the children to stick the boxes together to make a model. Young children will simply stick for the experience of using glue, slightly older children may name a model *after* they have made it. Even older children may set out to make a specific model.

Offer support and encouragement to children as they work on their models, but only help with specific tasks when asked to do so, or to prevent extreme frustration spoiling the child's participation in the activity. Adults can model useful techniques by making models alongside the children.

Extension

Leave the models to dry and then offer the children opportunities to paint or decorate them if they wish to.

Discussion

Encourage children to talk while they work creatively. Discuss the empty boxes and what they once held. Some will have contained substances with distinctive smells, such as tea, soap or herbs and spices. Ask children whether they can identify them by the smells and whether they like those original substances. Compare the sizes and colours of the packets and cartons and the types of writing that appears on them.